Such a Time As This

To my husband, Brian. Your simple gift of encouragement to me is also your extraordinary gift to the world.
Thank you for loving me.

TABLE OF CONTENTS

Introduction:
What is Advent?
How Do I Use This Book?

INTRODUCTION
What is Advent & How Do I Use This Book?

Advent is the preparation of our hearts for Jesus. Christians make intentional efforts each year, reserving the four weeks prior to Christmas as Advent season. The tradition is often set by lighting candles each week to guide the way of the coming of Christ. Advent is the dawning of what is to come. It is the intentionality of expectant prayer, reflection, and a reexamination of purpose in the Christian faith. Symbolically, we prepare our hearts for the birth of Jesus. Practically, we lay foundational work for our hearts to better reflect Jesus. But what does this mean in a world such as today, in a time such as this? How is Jesus relevant in a culture that consistently gets the message of Christ confused with doctrine, politics or morality? In a culture, whose own Christians muddle a simple faith into dogmatic disciplines of do's and don'ts, creating an uninviting table meant for all--how do we, then, center upon our hearts' preparation for Jesus?

This devotional is a guide for your Advent season. It attempts to challenge our theology, question our thought practices, and reengage the simple message of Jesus. It's a wonderful season to thoughtfully absorb what it means to be a Christ-follower in

Such a Time as This.

There are four chapters and four weeks of Advent. Each devotional is short, but the questions and action points to follow may require more time. You may engage as much or as little as you wish, but note that, as with all things, intentionality will create a deeper experience for your Advent preparation.

This devotional can be used as an individual study and as such can be beautifully self-engaging. Group study, however, is highly recommended. Reflecting in community can challenge us in ways that are both accountable and eye-opening to our faith journey. The insights of others can teach us something new about ourselves and our understanding of God. It can shine light on our biases and untruths and lead us deeper in our faith journey. Group work can be formal or informal. Gather friends, a bible study group, or one or two neighbors and commit to your readings and a simple discussion together.

Each chapter is comprised of a weekly devotional, followed by challenging questions and action points, a prayer and a quick reference summary page. Also included are lyrics to traditional hymn carols to accompany each weekly theme. If you are doing a group study, you might choose to close your session by singing the assigned hymn together. The lyrics to these old carols are both scriptural and beautiful. Additionally, there are plenty of blank pages to write your thoughts in each chapter and some additional note pages in the back.

Take your time through this journey. Nothing is more important than dedicating space to spiritual growth. Be intentional about the season so that your spiritual stretching is healthy and enriched.

Suggested Schedule of Readings

Below is a suggested schedule for working through this Advent devotional. Begin four weeks prior to Christmas on any chosen day of the week. Try to build this into your weekly rhythm by carving space in your calendar on the same day each week. Engage the content throughout the week as there are both questions and action points to challenge you. You may find spreading your reading out throughout the week is more helpful in absorbing the content, but work to complete the material within the week assigned.

Week 1 (first week of Advent): Read ***Rediscovering Hope***

Week 2 (second week of Advent): Read ***Redefining Peace***

Week 3 (third week of Advent): Read ***Reclaiming Joy***

Week 4 (fourth week of Advent): Read ***Restoring Love***

Week One:
Rediscovering Hope

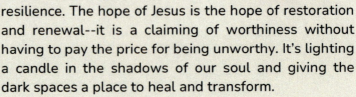

WEEK ONE
Rediscovering Hope

Hope. It allows us to look at the future with optimism. It launches us through difficult seasons, birthing strength and resilience. The hope of Jesus is the hope of restoration and renewal--it is a claiming of worthiness without having to pay the price for being unworthy. It's lighting a candle in the shadows of our soul and giving the dark spaces a place to heal and transform.

And yet there are seasons when claiming that hope is difficult. It is easier to burrow into hopelessness than to push ourselves toward a brighter day. There are seasons when we are nearly forced to rest in that space and to listen–to wait on a certain refinement that God is grinding out in us. In these dark spaces, when we do not necessarily feel hope, we must move towards the One who *is* Hope. When hope feels more like a fairytale than something you can taste and hold– we can lean into Christ for renewal and restoration.

There's another reason claiming hope can be difficult. When we attempt to manage the access to that hope, we make it difficult for people to know a loving, welcoming Christ. Despite a growing poor theology in our churches that we must be a certain way and follow certain rules in order to claim the hope of Christ, Jesus gives us hope and does so without stipulation. We mustn't be or do anything. In the darkest places of our lives, Christ sits in the mire with us. When we are in these spaces, we don't have the extra energy to do or be a certain way. We are where we are. Thank God the Gospel is simpler than we often portray it to be. It is for all that Christ came, right where we are. We are fully included, fully forgiven, and fully delivered. It is free. It is abundant. It is ours. We needn't do anything to be included in the hope of Jesus!

Jesus gives us hope and does so without stipulation.

As Christ-followers, we want to be mindful of how we package such a gift to others and ourselves. It's easy to package the gift of Jesus with shame. Culturally it is hard to imagine receiving such a gift without payment. But the Gospel of Jesus is a simple message that needn't be complicated by a list of rules or a blanket of guilt. This type of messaging not only narrows the table to which all are invited but is contrary to the very heart of the Gospel.

Shame is not of God. When people turn from the Church and God altogether, I wonder if many aren't turning from a fully inclusive, redeeming message but rather the packaging of that message from a passionate, but misguided church. Scriptures are not weapons. It is not up to us to say who is in and who is out. Many long for a meaningful spiritual connection. Are we the people who are attempting to manage access to what is meant for all?

The hope of redemption is Jesus alone. We are neither gatekeepers of the Gospel, nor have we been appointed its compliance officers. It is not a gift from us to them, but from God to all. It's important, as a Church and Christ-followers, that we rediscover the hope that is Jesus in a manner that is true to the spirit of the gift.

Free. And For All.
Accessible in whatever mire you find yourself sitting.

The simple message of the Gospel is hope. When we know we are included, forgiven, and delivered, the hope of Christ alone will heal and transform us. The light we shine comes not from our condemnation, but directly from reflecting Jesus in our living. It shines through in love, in joy, in peace, and in hope.

"Therefore, there is now no condemnation for those who are in Christ Jesus, because through Christ Jesus the law of the Spirit who gives life has set you free from the law of sin and death (shame)." Romans 8: 1-2

Practical Ways to Rediscovering Hope

- Remember your history. *What other moments in your past has the hope of Jesus rescued you?*
- Discern the cause of your hopelessness and seek help. *You are not alone.*
- Pray. Talk to God about your fears, concerns. *Tell God where you are drowning and ask God for rescue. Watch for it.*
- Know that you have purpose solely because you were created by a loving God. *Your value is immeasurable to your Creator.*
- Trust God to be creating in you beauty from ashes. There is hope, yet! *You have a God who loves you, just for being you, and loves you right where you are—even in the mire.*

Questions for Reflection

Describe your hope in Jesus. How has Christ's hope sustained you? Describe a season of hope.

Do you hold shame? Why or why not? How can you release any shame you hold?

Reexamine your understanding of hope in Jesus. Who has legitimate access to the hope you ascribe to? What do you expect of those ready to accept the hope of Jesus? Do you trust God to continue a redemptive work within them? Question whether your accountability involves shame. Question whether your judgement is stronger than

your mercy.

Rediscovering Hope

Quick Reference: The Relevance of Jesus for Hope

Jesus came to restore and redeem all.
The hope of Christ can renew the world.
We are fully accepted into the family.
We are fully redeemed.

In a world where many are rejected,

Jesus embraces all.

Jesus can offer hope in chaos, optimism in despair.
Christ gives us purpose to cling to, that we are not
overcome.

In a world where many feel overcome,

Jesus is present & conquers all.

Jesus gave his life to make eternal life possible for us.
We can hold onto this promise of hope, no matter
what this life brings.

In a world where many fear death,

Jesus unearths the dead and gives new life.

Action Points:

- **Trust the Hope that is Jesus.** Am I relying on the Holy Spirit to make me more like Jesus or am I trying to live holy by my own strength? Made up by my own rules? In the expectation of my church, my traditions, even my politics--rather than my God?

- **Engage your discomforts.** Where are you struggling at the table meant for all? Who are you uncomfortable sitting with? Get to know someone who thinks differently than you do, not for proving your points, but for listening. Learn about the person whom God also loves.

- **List practical ways** you can show God's hope this week. Many feel hopeless, but God's very message for humanity is hope! How can you show an authentic hope to others this week?

- **Submit your hopelessness to God.** What do I think is impossible in my life? Have I given up hope in the God of the Possible? Prayerfully consider the glimmer of hope that still shines within you.

Prayer

Thank You for the hope You give through Your Spirit. Help me to trust in Your promises and to hold fast to the hope that anchors my soul. May Your hope overflow in my life and spill out to those around me. Amen.

"May the God of hope fill you with all joy and peace as you trust in him, so that you may overflow with hope by the power of the Holy Spirit."
Romans 15:13

Rediscovering Hope

O Come, O Come Emmanuel

O come, O come, Emmanuel,
and ransom captive Israel
that mourns in lonely exile here
until the Son of God appear.

Refrain:
Rejoice! Rejoice! Emmanuel
shall come to you, O Israel.

O come, O Wisdom from on high,
who ordered all things mightily;
to us the path of knowledge show
and teach us in its ways to go. (refrain)

O come, O Branch of Jesse's stem,
unto your own and rescue them!
From depths of hell your people save,
and give them victory o'er the grave. (refrain)

O come, O Bright and Morning Star,
and bring us comfort from afar!
Dispel the shadows of the night
and turn our darkness into light. (refrain)

O come, O King of nations, bind
in one the hearts of all mankind.
Bid all our sad divisions cease
and be yourself our King of Peace. (refrain)

Neale, J.M. "O Come, O Come Emmanuel." (English translation of 9th century Latin hymn). 1851.

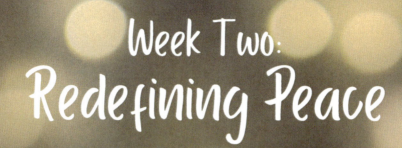

Week Two:
Redefining Peace

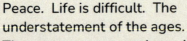

Peace. Life is difficult. The understatement of the ages. The seasons we experience in one lifetime are enough to bring heartache, anxiety, fear, depression, apprehension, skepticism and a wealth of pain. And yet there is a peace that can sustain us through these seasons; a knowing that we are going to be okay; a resting in the security that we are loved by our Creator. The peace, or shalom, of Christ does not keep us from the chaos, but settles us within it. Being still is often associated with the peace of Jesus. Mark 4 tells the story of Jesus rebuking the winds and the waves.

"He got up, rebuked the wind and said to the waves, 'Quiet (*Siope*)! Be still.' Then the wind died down and it was completely calm." Mark 4:39

The Greek word *siope*, translated as *peace* in many translations, is really used as a command to the winds and waves to settle. Jesus takes the rage of the sea and silences its voice. *Siope*. Quiet. Peace. Be still. Nothing can speak stronger into our chaos than Christ.

So what happens when our deepest fears are met? When tragedy claims our loved ones too soon? When sickness beckons us to come a little closer? When abuse is at the center of our lives? When relationships end? These are real situations where peace feels elusive and chaos all consuming. Where is God's peace in those deep waters? What do we do when we feel Jesus is asleep in the storm? *Call out for help.*

Wake Jesus up with your tears and your fears! I can't tell you how many times I've dropped to my knees in puddles of despair. *Wake up, Jesus! Calm the storms within me!*

Draw into the community of Christ, your village. The disciples, too, believed they were perishing, but Christ is still commanding the winds and the waves today. Have faith Jesus is in your boat! Be brave to draw near and know the shalom of Christ. Christ will command the storms to settle within you so that you may face the chaos with Jesus firmly in your boat.

Questions for Reflection

How do you feel about waking Jesus up? Jesus can handle your pain, your anger, your terror. Do you believe this?

Who is your village? Who would you go to if you needed help claiming the peace of Christ?

Are you the village for others? Do you serve as an extension of the Peacemaker or are you the wind and waves? Consider the words you use, how you communicate on social media, how you speak about and to those with whom you disagree. God does not need your defense. God needs your peacemaking. How can you be a better peacemaker? **25**

Redefining Peace

Quick Reference: The Relevance of Jesus for Peace

The peace of Jesus is superior to the peace of the world. We can be fully in the storm, but still have peace within.

In a world of many storms,

the peace of Jesus is available to us.

The peace of Jesus creates unity among enemies.

In a world where division is widespread,

Jesus unites.

The peace of Jesus is with us and fully realized upon our full surrender to Christ.

In a world of loneliness, fear, and despair

Jesus gives assurance he is with us.

Action Points:

- *Siope*. Peace, be still. **Use this word as a mantra** when you encounter unrest to remind yourself that Jesus still commands the winds and waves. Write it on sticky notes for your mirror, car dash, work desk, refrigerator.

- **Ask God** to help you identify your restlessness. Where are you trying to control life? Submit this to God and seek intervention. Ask for peace to preside well over your need to control.

- **Practice being a peacemaker.** When situations arise that fire up your instinct to argue, **pause**. Ask yourself how you can respond as a peacemaker, how you can reflect the peace of Christ to others?

Prayer

Thank You for Your peace that surpasses all understanding. Help me to trust You relentlessly and to rest in the assurance that You are in control. Fill me with Your peace today, and let it overflow into every area of my life. Amen.

"And the peace of God, which transcends all understanding, will guard your hearts and your minds in Christ Jesus." Philippians 4:7

Redefining Peace

It Came Upon The Midnight Clear

It came upon the midnight clear,
that glorious song of old,
from angels bending near the earth
to touch their harps of gold:
"Peace on the earth, good will to men,
from heaven's all-gracious King."
The world in solemn stillness lay,
to hear the angels sing.

And ye, beneath life's crushing load,
whose forms are bending low,
who toil along the climbing way
with painful steps and slow,
look now! for glad and golden hours
come swiftly on the wing.
O rest beside the weary road,
and hear the angels sing!

For lo! the days are hastening on,
by prophet seen of old,
when with the ever-circling years
shall come the time foretold
when peace shall over all the earth
its ancient splendors fling,
and the whole world send back the song
which now the angels sing.

Week Three:
Reclaiming Joy

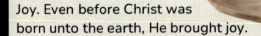

Joy. Even before Christ was born unto the earth, He brought joy.

"When Elizabeth heard Mary's greeting, the baby leaped in her womb, and Elizabeth was filled with the Holy Spirit. In a loud voice she exclaimed: 'Blessed are you among women, and blessed is the child you will bear! ...As soon as the sound of your greeting reached my ears, the baby in my womb leaped for joy.'" Luke 1: 41-44

Jesus is joy! He is the good news that has come for all people (Luke 2:10-11). And that joy is our strength (Nehemiah 8:10). It is our strength because we can rely upon its promises of presence, redemption, and restoration for all. Even in the midst of seasons where nothing feels joyful, Jesus IS.

I struggle in Joy. I often confuse it with happiness and Joy is not happiness. You can have Joy and not be happy. Many of us are subject to the wiles of depression. These are real places in our spirits, real demons we battle. The best way I can separate my understanding between joy and happiness is by reclaiming gratitude in my life and combining this with praise. This is Joy.

To know Christ is to know God is with you.
To know Christ is to know you are fully worthy.
To know Christ is to know hope, full redemption, full restoration! Even in dark places. And this is joy!

What we know about Joy

- Joy comes when we live in God's presence (Psalm 21:5-7).
- As we abide in Christ, we express this fruit of joy more and more (John 15:5).
- Joy comes when we praise God, expressing gratitude for what God has already done (Psalm 92:4-5).
- God is able to restore our joy when we feel it is lost (Psalm 94:19).
- No one can take away your joy (John 16:22).
- We can experience and encourage joy in community (Ecclesiastes 4:9–12).
- There is an "inexpressible and glorious joy" inside of you (1 Peter 1:8).

Questions for Reflection

Describe a time when you most recognized this Joy of the Lord. What were you doing? Who was with you? If you've never recognized this Joy, take a moment to ask God to restore the Joy within you. You are worthy because God says you are worthy, without stipulation. The Joy belongs to you.

How can you reclaim Joy when you feel it is lost to you?
Recall what you know of Joy.

How do you share Joy with others? Do people know you carry Joy? Why or why not? How can you better express the Joy of Christ to others?

Quick Reference: The Relevance of Jesus for Joy

The Joy of Jesus is Χαρά (greek pronounced khar-ah meaning "calm delight"). This Joy is a praise and gratitude for who Christ is and what Christ has done for us.

In a world of fleeting happiness,
Jesus offers abundant joy.

As we express our praise & gratitude, live in generous community together, and spend time in God's presence, we can know the Joy of Jesus.

In a world that destroys,
Jesus restores. Your joy can be restored.

Joy is yours and Joy is mine.

In a world that takes,
The Joy of Jesus stays.
No one can take your Joy.

Action Points:

- ***Practice being in the presence of God.*** Take time to notice small, simple joys that God brings to you daily. Build this into your weekly rhythm. This can look like a quiet walk, journaling, sitting on your porch or at a park, etc. Take time to listen, to be still in the presence of God.

- **Begin a gratitude journal.** Naming our thanksgivings is a wonderful way to remember God seeks to bring us joy. Write one thing you are grateful for each day. We can praise God for what God has already done in our lives. We can praise God in the anticipation for blessings to come.

- **Engage with community.** Share joys and burdens with people. This can increase our joy. We are reminded God is working when we share together in community. What is one way you can engage with others this week?

Prayer

Thank You for the gift of Your joy. Help me to find my strength in You, especially when life feels difficult. Let Your joy within me be a source of strength and encouragement to others. May Your joy be evident in my life today. Amen.

"The joy of the Lord is your strength."
Nehemiah 8:10

Reclaiming Joy

Reclaiming Joy

Joy to the World

Joy to the World

Joy to the world, the Lord is come!
Let earth receive her King!
Let every heart prepare Him room,
and heav'n and nature sing,
and heav'n and nature sing,
and heav'n, and heav'n and nature sing.

Joy to the earth, the Savior reigns!
Let men their songs employ,
while fields and floods, rocks, hills, and plains
repeat the sounding joy,
repeat the sounding joy,
repeat, repeat the sounding joy.

No more let sins and sorrows grow,
nor thorns infest the ground;
He comes to make His blessings flow
far as the curse is found,
far as the curse is found,
far as, far as the curse is found.

He rules the world with truth and grace,
and makes the nations prove
the glories of His righteousness
and wonders of His love,
and wonders of His love,
and wonders, wonders of His love.

Watts, Isaac. "Joy to the World." 1719.

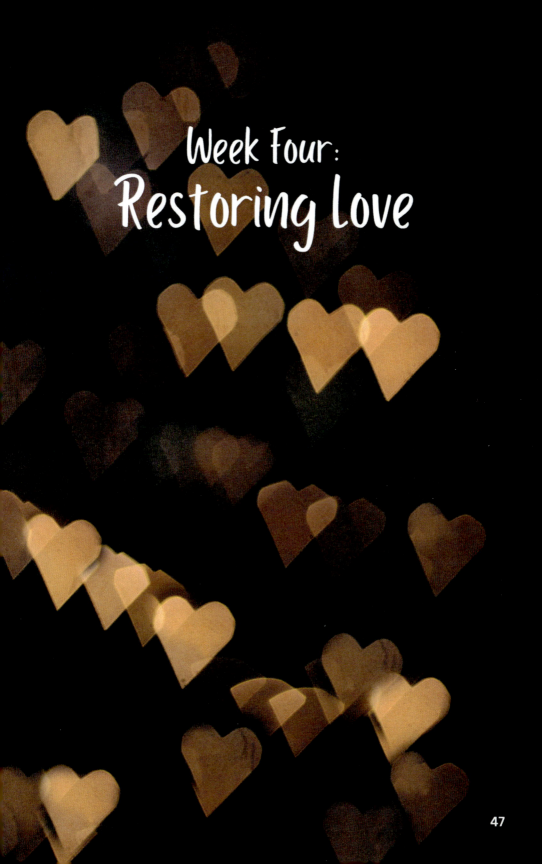

Week Four:
Restoring Love

WEEK FOUR
Restoring Love

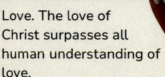

Love. The love of Christ surpasses all human understanding of love.

Parents know a fierce love for their children; God's love is even more relentless. Spouses love each other through many different seasons. Their love changes and grows, ebbs and flows. Christ's love is abundantly deeper.

We have a love for our family and a love for our friends. We have a love for food, hobbies, passions, and our pets. It's hard to comprehend a love that could be so much richer than what we already know love to be.

And yet our understanding and our practice of love can be conditional or temporary even as we hope it is not. Our temporal love can bring pain, abuse, manipulation, misunderstanding, or grief even if it is not our intention.

God gives us a love that is unwavering, unchanging, and eternal. It is a love that says "you are enough." It is a love that is, in and of itself, enough. And a love that beckons us near when we feel unlovely, unworthy, and unredeemable. It is this steadfast, unfailing, transforming love that came to us in the beginning and continues to stay with us long after the birth, ministry, death and resurrection of Jesus. God so loved, so loved the world.

For God so loved the world that he gave his one and only Son, that whoever believes in him shall not perish but have eternal life."
John 3:16

Still, it is hard to love people. People carry baggage and baggage gets heavy. People can be unlovely and unlovable. The good news is that God's transforming love overflows! The abundance is produced of Holy Spirit power. The moment we embrace God's restorative and life-changing love, it empowers us to connect with others more deeply than we ever thought possible. This love is as fresh as each sunrise, faithful and renewable.

Years ago we welcomed a small boy into our family. His mother, for reasons known only to her, felt her best option was to place her child into our family. From the beginning, I was determined to love him. My love for him grew so fierce I often forget I did not bear him myself. But I often worried I wouldn't be enough for him. As the years passed and my love for all four of my children deepened, I found myself increasingly afraid of failing them, each for different reasons. The worry became my focus. Then a friend gently reminded me that I could never be **all things** for **any** of my children. My love, no matter how fervent, would never be enough.

I sat with this stark truth. I understood her point, even as at the time I didn't like her point. It made me sharply aware of my self-reliance and my *inability to be full in anything without Christ.* My love had shifted from Christ-centered to performance-based (my own performance). I found my anchor loosely planted on *my* abilities rather than God's.

My love could never be enough, but God's love would. There is great freedom in knowing this and with a shift in focus, my fears were vanquished. Isn't this why Christ came? To set us free? The more we release our self-reliance, especially in our loving of others, the more we can love with the overflow of Christ's love in us. The best kind of love!

The love of Jesus is not performance-based but flows freely from Christ's very nature. Therefore, our overflow of Christ's love need not be performance-based, but gracious and merciful and fully connected to the Vine. We are dearly loved. We love others because God first loved us. It is the only way to love fully.

When we struggle to love ourselves or others, we can rest in the truth that we are already fully loved by God. We know this from Hope, we feel this from Peace, and we exude this as Joy. This full love is our anchor and our assurance that God is with us, Emmanuel.

Imagine a world where people simply surrendered this self-reliance. Imagine accepting freedom from whatever enslaves us and authentically praising God for such love! The love that sets us free! What a world it would be for all of us to love with the abundant love of Jesus--where we see people as fully included, fully forgiven, and fully redeemed! Where grace and compassion outshines all else!

Practical ways to love others with the love of Christ

- Accept people for who they are, where they are (Romans 15:7).

- Listen without interruption (Proverbs 18:13).

- Forgive without retaliation (Colossians 3:13).

- Avoid arguing (2 Timothy 2:23-26).

- Avoid accusations (James 1:19).

- Practice humility (Philippians 2:3-4).

- Be patient and kind (1 Corinthians 13:4).

- Be generous of self, time, and resources (Proverbs 21:26).

It is for freedom that Christ has set us free. Galatians 5:1

Questions for Reflection

Where do you find yourself enslaved? What holds you captive? This could be bad habits, but it could be subtler than this: self-reliance, control, captivity to our rhythms and routines, burdened by our anxieties of doing something wrong or not getting something quite right, etc. What enslaves you? What keeps you from accepting the freedom that God's love offers? Ask God to help you identify this entrapment. Then accept release from this. For Christ came to set you free, not keep you in slavery. And this is the epitome of love.

In our freedom, we can better love with the love of Christ because we know what entrapment feels like. We have more mercy, more grace, more understanding for others. Our mercy overflows because we've shifted our focus from behaving as *gatekeepers* of Christ's love to praising *God* as the Giver of love. What does loving others look like when you shift the center of your focus? What does freedom feel like when you shift the center of your focus?

Restorative love can only come from Christ. Do you need a reset? Christ's love is new every morning. You are dearly loved. Write a list of ways you see Christ's love over you and your life. Praise God for this restorative, abiding love. It sets us free!

Restoring Love

Quick Reference: The Relevance of Jesus for Love

The love of Jesus surpasses all other loves.

In a world of conditional love,
Jesus gives love everlasting.
The love of Christ is boundless and for all.

The love of Jesus overpours and is contagious.

In a world where love is finite,
the love of Christ is infinitely overflowing.
There is enough, because Christ alone is enough.

The love of Jesus restores what is broken.

In a world of broken people, relationships, and difficult
situations, the love of Christ creates beauty from ashes.

Action Points:

- **Identify who you struggle to love.** Ask God to change your heart for those individuals or groups of people. Ask God to help you eliminate biases, stereotypes, and hatred for others. Ask God to help you value their differences or find common ground. Practice refocusing your self-reliant love to Holy Spirit powered love.

- **Establish healthy boundaries.** Loving others does not mean harming self. Ask God and others in your community to help you establish healthy boundaries and safe havens should you be in harmful or unsafe relationships.

- **Love your community.** Choose a day this month to volunteer your time serving others: Soup kitchens, clothing closets, food banks, shelters, schools, etc. Step out of your comfort zone and try something new. Serving others can deepen our ability to love.

- **Allow someone to love you.** You are worthy. Say 'thank you' for the gift *without* feeling bad you didn't give them one. Appreciate the compliment without making an excuse for it. If you need assistance in this season, **ask for it**. Allow someone to love you. People have a greater capacity for love than we often realize and everyone needs love. Accept it from your village.

Prayer

Thank You for Your steadfast love. Help me to embrace the truth that Your love never fails and that I am fully known and fully loved by You, fully accepted and fully redeemed. May Your love transform me and pour out over others. Amen.

"Because of the LORD's great love we are not consumed, for his compassions never fail. They are new every morning; great is your faithfulness."
Lamentations 3:22-23

Restoring Love

O Holy Night

O holy night! the stars are brightly shining;
It is the night of the dear Savior's birth.
Long lay the world in sin and error pining,
Till He appeared and the soul felt its worth.
A thrill of hope- the weary world rejoices,
For yonder breaks a new and glorious morn!
Fall on your knees! O hear the angel voices!
O night divine, O night when Christ was born!
O night, O holy night, O night divine!

Led by the light of faith serenely beaming,
With glowing hearts by His cradle we stand.
So led by light of a star sweetly gleaming,
Here came the Wise Men from Orient land.
The King of kings lay thus in lowly manger,
In all our trials born to be our Friend.
He knows our need— to our weakness is no stranger.
Behold your King, before Him lowly bend!
Behold your King, before Him lowly bend!

Truly He taught us to love one another;
His law is love and His gospel is peace.
Chains shall He break, for the slave is our brother,
And in His name all oppression shall cease.
Sweet hymns of joy in grateful chorus raise we;
Let all within us praise His holy name.
Christ is the Lord! O praise His name forever!
His pow'r and glory evermore proclaim!
His pow'r and glory evermore proclaim!

Cappeau, Placide. "O Holy Night." (original French lyrics), 1843.
Dwight, John Sullivan. "O Holy Night." (English translation), 1855.
©Public Domain

Notes from the Author
A Challenge for Us All

My exercise in writing is often to say something to myself. When I'm brave enough to publish, I hope that other people find value in it and are challenged in ways that only God can prompt. I wrote this devotional book as a practice of recalling a simple faith--the faith that says

Jesus is enough.

There's a strange movement of complexity brewing within our churches and our body of believers. It's a dangerous, unnecessary complexity. I think Paul would have letters stamped and mailed by now to each of us, pleading with us that Jesus is enough --that we needn't add to in order to make Christ relevant or ourselves or others worthier. We needn't decide what is holy and what is not for other people. For this is the work of the Holy Spirit, not holier than thou's. In the end, we believe ourselves to be doing something right for the church, but in reality, we are narrowing the table to which all are invited and attempting to defend the God who needs no defense from the imperfect.

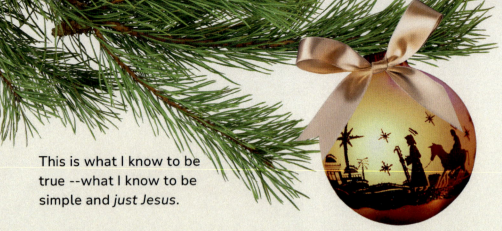

This is what I know to be true --what I know to be simple and *just Jesus*.

- God sent Jesus to be among us, to live a life of example and to fulfill scripture.

- Jesus turned our understanding of scripture on its ends and we realized, along with the disciples, that what we thought we knew--we did not. Therefore, we err on the side of grace, mercy, and humility as we walk together in community because it is futile to pretend we know all things.

- Jesus came for all, without stipulation. All. And he did not employ a gatekeeper to regulate this. Jesus came for all. All have access, which is why the message is simple and needs to be kept simple.

- The hope of Jesus is love, redemption, and inclusion. We are fully loved, fully redeemed, fully included.

- The peace of Jesus is his presence.

- The joy of Jesus is our strength.

- The love of Jesus is a gift to the world.

Thank you for taking this Advent journey with me. I hope you were richly blessed by your reflections and steps towards a deeper faith. I ask this of you as you close out one year and step into the next: Remember the simplicity that is the Gospel of Jesus. If we must preach a return to Christ to anyone, Dear God, let it be ourselves.

A New Year Focus

Write down one area of spiritual growth you feel particularly
nudged to focus on this upcoming year.

What specific actions do you need to take in order to step
into these challenges and deepen your faith journey? Pray
about this and write it down.

☐

☐

☐

☐

☐

Post this in a place where you can engage it *daily* for the upcoming year.

Notes

Notes

Notes

Notes

Notes

Notes

Notes

Notes

Notes